Little
WORD WHIZZ

Animal Words for Little ZOOLOGISTS

Will Millard

Monika Forsberg

MAGIC CAT PUBLISHING

Words Words Words

This book contains one hundred words to help young zoologists better understand the natural world around them.

Some words shine a light on the amazing abilities that animals have and the extraordinary things they can do: **camouflage**, **regenerate**, **metamorphosis**!

Others explain an animal's role in nature and the relationship it has to the world around it: **pollinator**, **apex predator**.

Many of the words form opposite pairs: **predator** and **prey**, **arboreal** and **terrestrial**, **herbivore** and **carnivore**.

Altogether, these words paint an amazing picture of how everything in nature is connected and has its place.

And as we better understand the natural world, we come to care for it more and understand our place in nature, too.

| What do these words mean? | **Larva** The young form of an animal that undergoes metamorphosis. | **Spawn** The eggs of an amphibian, such as a frog, and also fish. | **Metamorphosis** The transformation that some animals, like frogs, go through to become an adult. |

| **Mature** Fully developed, with all its physical adult features in place. | **Moult** The stage when a dragonfly larva leaves its case and emerges an adult. | Can you spot these five things? **Frog** • **Goose** • **Tadpole** • **Pike** • **Dragonfly** • |

What do these words mean?

Terrestrial
An animal that spends most of its time on the ground, as the panda does.

Fossorial
An animal that is good at digging and spends much of its life underground.

Crest
The tuft of feathers sometimes present on a bird's head.

Arboreal
An animal that spends most of its time living among the trees.

Litter
A group of baby animals that were born at the same time to the same mother.

Can you spot these five things?
Panda • **Bamboo rat** • **Golden pheasant** • **Black bear** • **Golden snub-nosed monkey**

What do these words mean?

Proboscis
A long, flexible or tube-like nose used for sucking.

Pollinator
An animal, often an insect, that carries pollen from one plant to another.

Spinneret
A spider's silk-spinning organ, at the base of its abdomen.

Crepuscular
Most active at dawn or dusk.

Radula
The thousands of tiny teeth with which snails and slugs eat.

Can you spot these five things?
Butterfly • **Bumblebee** • **Mouse** • **Spider** • **Snail** •

What do these words mean?

Territorial
An animal that wants to guard or defend the area where it lives.

Tentacle
Long, flexible limbs used for feeling, holding and catching food, and moving.

Gill
The organ that allows fish to take in oxygen from water.

Polyps
A tiny organism that clusters in a colony to form coral.

Carapace
The domed upper-part of a turtle or tortoise's hard, protective shell.

Can you spot these five things?
Clownfish • Octopus • Manta ray • Coral • Green turtle •

What do these words mean?

Camouflage
An animal's colours and patterns that make it hard to spot in its surroundings.

Herd
A large group of animals – usually hoofed mammals, like buffalo.

Herbivore
An animal that eats a diet of plants.

Carnivore
An animal that eats a diet of meat from other animals.

Tusk
An extra-long tooth, which some mammals – including elephants – have.

Can you spot these five things?
Leopard • **Buffalo** • **Lion** • **Rhinoceros** • **Elephant** •

What do these words mean?

Silverback
An adult male gorilla that grows silver hair on its back.

Social
An animal that lives together with others of its kind in a group.

Primate
A group of mammals that includes apes, monkeys and humans.

Endemic
A species found in only one place or part of the world, such as the okapi.

Solitary
An animal that spends most of its life on its own.

Can you spot these five things?
Gorilla • **Okapi** • **Chimpanzee** • **Colobus monkey** • **Pangolin** •

| What do these words mean? | **Nocturnal** Active at night and asleep during the day. | **Insectivore** An animal whose diet is made up mostly of insects. | **Omnivore** An animal, like a badger, that eats both plants and other animals. |

Omnivore

Limbless

Hibernate

Limbless	**Hibernate**	Can you spot these five things?
An animal that has no arms or legs.	To go into a sleep-like state for a long time, usually through winter.	**Badger • Owl • Shrew • Earthworm • Hedgehog •**

What do these words mean?

Prehensile
Able to grasp things – for instance, a monkey has a prehensile tail.

Poisonous
Contains a toxin that might be eaten, absorbed through skin or breathed in.

Venomous
Contains a toxin that might be delivered via a sting or a bite.

Rodent
A family of mammals including mice, rats, rabbits and capybaras!

Ambush
To attack prey by surprise, usually after hiding and waiting.

Can you spot these five things?
Gibbon • **Poison dart frog** • **Capybara** • **Pit viper** • **Jaguar**

What do these words mean?

Predator
An animal that hunts other animals and eats them.

Hoard
A stash of food hidden away by an animal to be eaten later.

Prey
An animal that is hunted by a predator for food.

Domestic

Pedigree
An animal descended from a pure line of parents of the same breed.

Domestic
Bred and tamed to live with humans, usually as a pet.

Can you spot these five things?
Hamster • Cat • Dog • Mouse • Rabbit •

What do these words mean?

Crustacean
A shelled creature with lots of pairs of legs, such as a crab, lobster or prawn.

Aquatic
An animal that lives all or most of its life in the water.

Microhabitat
A small area, like a rock pool, where animals live together.

Mollusc
A creature with a soft body often protected by a hard shell.

Regenerate
The ability to regrow a damaged or missing body part.

Can you spot these five things?
Crab • Prawn • Mussel • Starfish • Sea anemone •

Warm-blooded

Quadruped

Cold-blooded

What do these words mean?

Warm-blooded
An animal that keeps its body temperature constant by itself.

Cold-blooded
An animal that can't control its body temperature and relies on heat from the sun.

Quadruped
An animal that hops, runs or walks on four legs and has four feet.

Biped

Arthropod

Arthropod
An animal that has jointed legs and no backbone.

Biped
An animal that hops, runs or walks on two legs and has two feet.

Can you spot these five things?
Camel • **Ostrich** • **Scorpion** • **Monitor lizard** • **Dung beetle** •

What do these words mean?

Marsupial
A group of mammals whose mothers carry their young babies in a pouch.

Monotreme
The only kind of mammal to lay eggs, found in Australia and New Guinea.

Scale
Horny or bony overlapping plates that cover the skin of reptiles and fish.

Joey
A baby kangaroo or other young marsupial.

Burrow
A hole or tunnel dug by an animal for it to live in.

Can you spot these five things?
Koala • **Platypus** • **Kangaroo** • **Thorny devil** • **Wombat** •

What do these words mean?

Pup
A baby of certain mammals, including seals, rats and dogs.

Polar
Living in the area around the North or South poles.

Salt water
Water that contains salt, especially sea or ocean water.

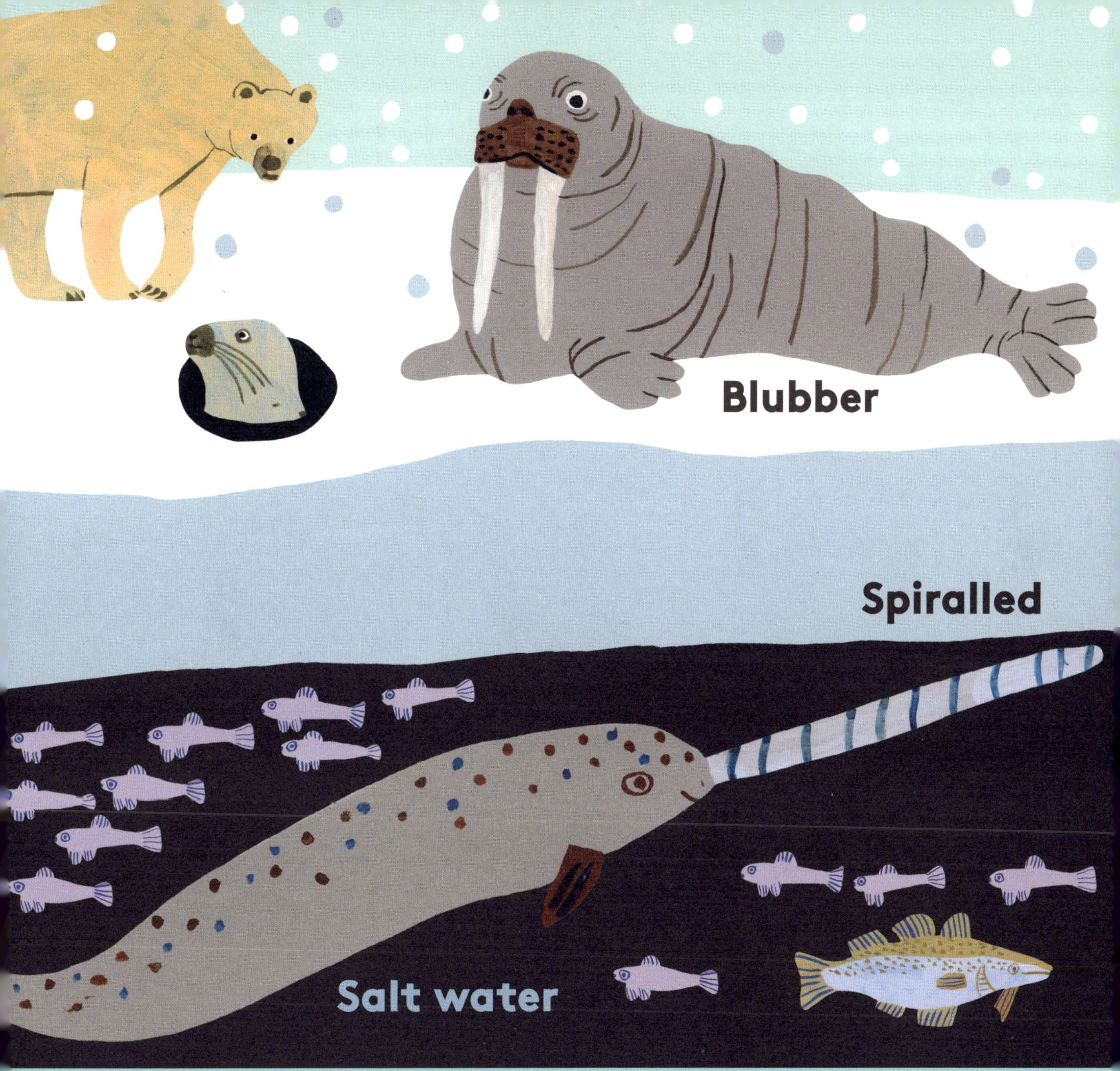

Blubber

Spiralled

Salt water

Blubber
The thick layer of fat that keeps sea mammals warm.

Spiralled
Twisted, coiled or winded.

Can you spot these five things?
Seal • **Polar bear** • **Cod** • **Narwhal** • **Walrus** •

Huddle

Baleen

Plankton

| What do these words mean? | **Huddle** To nestle closely together for warmth. | **Plankton** Microscopic creatures, such as krill, which drift or float in the sea. | **Baleen** Hairy filters used by animals like whales to strain tiny food from seawater. |

Flightless

Apex predator

Flightless
An animal that is unable to fly, despite having wing-like limbs.

Apex predator
The very top hunting animal, which has no natural predators.

Can you spot these five things?
Penguin • **Chick** • **Krill** • **Whale** • **Orca** •

Wader

Plumage

Antennae

What do these words mean?

Antennae
The long, thin feelers that some invertebrates have.

Wader
A type of bird commonly found stalking through shallow waters.

Plumage
A bird's feathers altogether.

Flippers
Broad, flat limbs used by water animals for swimming.

Courtship
Behaviour that aims to attract a mate to make babies with.

Can you spot these five things?
Heron • **Lobster** • **Seagrass** • **Manatee** • **Seahorse** •

What do these words mean?

Cartilaginous
A creature with a skeleton made of rubbery cartilage and not hard bone.

Bait-ball
A ball-shaped, very densely packed shoal of fish, which is used for defence.

Fin
A flattened body part that sticks out and helps a fish to swim.

Pod
A group of ocean animals such as dolphins or whales.

Glide
To fly through the air without flapping wings.

Can you spot these five things?
Shark • **Sardine** • **Sailfish** • **Albatross** • **Dolphin** •

Talon

What do these words mean?

Talon
The sharp claws of an animal, especially a bird of prey.

Antler
Bony extension that grows from the head of a male deer, like a moose.

Cub
A young meat-eating mammal, such as a bear, lion or fox.

Migration
Seasonal movement by animals over a long distance to find food or to reproduce.

Fresh water
Water that does not contain salt, found in many rivers and lakes.

Can you spot these five things?
Wolf • **Bald eagle** • **Moose** • **Salmon** • **Grizzly bear** •

| What do these words mean? | **Bovine** An animal from the cattle family, including cows, buffalo and bison. | **Swine** A word also used for pig. | **Fleece** The woolly coat of a sheep. |

Poultry
Birds kept and raised by humans for their meat or eggs, such as geese or chickens.

Equine
An animal from the horse family, including horses, zebras and donkeys.

Can you spot these five things?
Cow • Pig • Sheep • Chicken • Horse •

What do these words mean?

Forager
An animal that searches widely for food, such as fruit, to eat.

Endangered
An animal with so few of its type left that it might disappear forever.

Forked
Something with a divided end, like a snake's tongue.

Mimic
An animal that imitates something else to hide and avoid being hunted.

Ungulate
A varied group of hoofed mammals, including pigs, horses and tapirs.

Can you spot these five things?
Orangutan • **Tiger** • **Python** • **Tapir** • **Stick insect** •

39

| What do these words mean? | **Bask**
 To lie in the sun's heat to warm up. | **Adaptation**
 A feature, like a giraffe's long neck, which develops through evolution. | **Waterhole**
 A dip in the ground containing water, which animals visit to drink from. |

Semiaquatic
An animal that lives partly on land, and partly in water.

Flock
A group of birds.

Can you spot these five things?
Crocodile • Hyena • Giraffe • Zebra • Hippopotamus •

Invertebrates

Invertebrates are a huge collection of animals that all share one thing in common – they do not have a backbone. Instead they have hard bodies, which protect their organs. Ninety-seven per cent of all animals are invertebrates!

Here are some of the different kinds you'll find:

Insects
These creatures have three pairs of legs, jointed bodies and a pair of antennae. Most insects have wings, too.

Gastropods
All gastropods have a single muscular foot and a pair of tentacles. Many, like snails, have a shell, but some, like slugs, do not.

Arachnids
Spiders, scorpions and mites are the most common arachnids. They have four pairs of legs and many are venomous.

Cephalopods
Sea-living creatures including squid, octopus and cuttlefish. They have large bodies and a set of tentacles.

Crustaceans
Crabs, lobsters and shrimps are the best-known crustaceans. They all have hard shells and most live in water.

Fish

Fish fill our waters around the world, from huge salty oceans to small freshwater streams and ponds. This group of animals are cold-blooded and live exclusively in the water.

Here are some of the features we see in fish:

Swim bladders
Most fish have this organ, which stops them from sinking – or floating! – in the water.

Tails
Fish use their tails to swim.

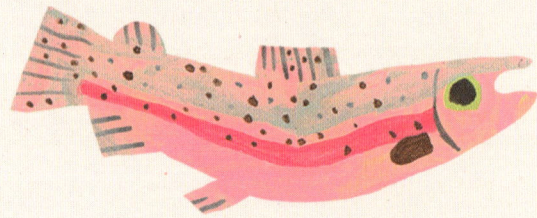

Gills
Fish can breathe underwater thanks to their gills.

Fins
Fish have fins that help them manoeuvre in the water.

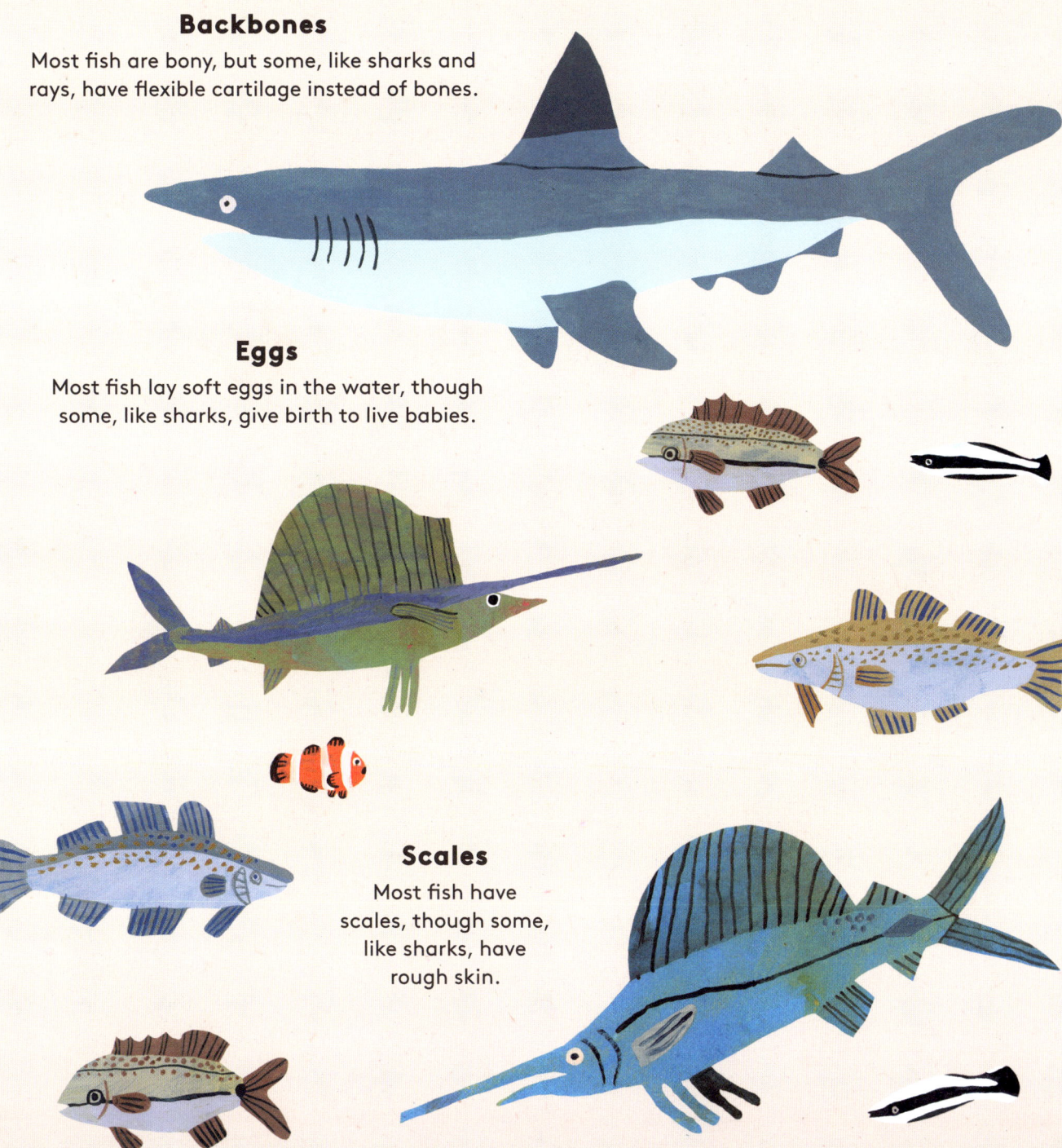

Amphibians

The amphibian family includes frogs and toads, newts, caecilians and axolotls. These cold-blooded animals live partly on land and partly in water. They are especially abundant in rainforests, where they are suited to the warm, damp climate.

Here are some of the features we see in amphibians:

Backbones
Amphibians are vertebrates with a backbone.

Lungs
Adult amphibians breathe air through their lungs.

Moist skin
Amphibians have smooth, moist skin, which they are also able to breathe through.

Eggs
Baby amphibians hatch from soft eggs, which the adults lay in fresh water.

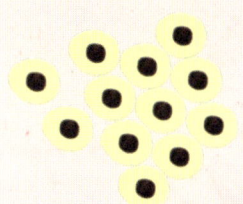

Metamorphosis
As it grows, an amphibian's body transforms and grows legs that allow it to move on land.

Four legs
Most amphibians grow four legs.

Reptiles

The reptile family includes snakes, iguanas, lizards, geckos, turtles, chameleons, crocodiles and alligators. These cold-blooded animals live mostly on land and are found all over the world where it is warm enough.

Here are some of the features we see in reptiles:

Scales
Instead of fur or feathers, reptiles have scales.

Legs
Most reptiles have four legs, though snakes have none!

Tails
All reptiles have a tail.

Lungs
Reptiles breathe air through their lungs.

Eggs
Baby reptiles hatch from eggs with leathery shells.

Backbones
Reptiles are vertebrates with a backbone.

Ancestors
Scientists think that birds and mammals both evolved from reptile ancestors, which is why they have many features in common.

Birds

Birds are easy to spot thanks to their distinctive wings and feathers. These warm-blooded creatures live all around the world, filling our skies and oceans, and covering the land, too.

Here are some of the features we see in birds:

Lungs
Birds breathe air through their lungs.

Feathers
Birds are covered with feathers that keep them warm and help them to fly.

Beaks
All birds have beaks and no teeth.

Backbones
Birds are vertebrates with a backbone.

Tails
All birds have a tail.

Wings
Many birds use their wings to fly, but others, such as penguins, use them to swim.

Legs
Birds have two legs.

Eggs
Baby chicks hatch from eggs with hard shells. The parents usually lay eggs in a nest and incubate them (sit on them to keep them warm until the chicks hatch).

Mammals

Mammals are warm-blooded, and stay cosy thanks to their distinctive fur. They live across the globe, on land and in water, from the freezing polar oceans to the hottest deserts. Humans have lots in common with these creatures because we are also mammals!

Here are some of the features we see in mammals:

Milk
Mothers produce milk to feed their young.

Live young
All mammals give birth to live young, except platypuses and echidnas, which lay eggs.

Backbones
Mammals are vertebrates with a backbone.

Tails
All mammals have a tail, except for us humans!

Fur
Mammals have fur or hair to protect their skin and keep them warm.

Legs
All land mammals have four legs, while water-based mammals have evolved to have flippers.

Lungs
Mammals breathe air through their lungs – even those that live underwater.

MAGIC CAT PUBLISHING

Little Word Whizz: Animal Words for Little Zoologists © 2024 Lucky Cat Publishing Ltd
Written by Will Millard
Text © 2024 Lucky Cat Publishing Ltd
Illustrations © 2024 Monika Forsberg
First Published in 2024 by Magic Cat Publishing, an imprint of Lucky Cat Publishing Ltd,
Unit 2 Empress Works, 24 Grove Passage, London E2 9FQ, UK

The right of Monika Forsberg to be identified as the illustrator of this work has been asserted by them in accordance with the Copyright, Designs and Patents Act, 1988 (UK).

No part of this publication may be reproduced, stored in a retrieval system, or transmitted, in any form, or by any means, electrical, mechanical, photocopying, recording or otherwise without the prior written permission of the publisher or a licence permitting restricted copying.

A catalogue record for this book is available from the British Library.

ISBN 978-1-915569-43-1

The illustrations were painted with gouache and composed digitally
Set in Brown and School Hand

Published by Rachel Williams and Jenny Broom
Designed by Nicola Price

Manufactured in China

9 8 7 6 5 4 3 2 1